Linda, Thank ~~you so~~ much for
help ~~~~ ial.
~~~~ Love,
Cissy 2024

THE
SHEPHERD
AND THE
LAMB

THE
SHEPHERD
AND THE
LAMB

OUR COVENANT HOPE IN CHRIST

GERRIT W. GONG

SALT LAKE CITY, UTAH

© 2024 Gerrit W. Gong

All rights reserved. No part of this book may be reproduced in any form or by any means without permission in writing from the publisher, Deseret Book Company, at permissions@deseretbook.com. This work is not an official publication of The Church of Jesus Christ of Latter-day Saints. The views expressed herein are the responsibility of the author and do not necessarily represent the position of the Church or of Deseret Book Company.

DESERET BOOK is a registered trademark of Deseret Book Company.

Visit us at deseretbook.com

Library of Congress Cataloging-in-Publication Data
CIP on file
ISBN 978-1-63993-268-9

Printed in the United States of America
Publishers Printing, Salt Lake City, UT

10   9   8   7   6   5   4   3   2   1

For and with SLG

CONTENTS

Preface | ix
Introduction: The Shepherd and the Lamb | 1

PART ONE
THE GOOD SHEPHERD
Our Guide and Exemplar | 8

Chapter 1: He Calls | 11
Chapter 2: He Gathers | 21
Chapter 3: He Ministers | 31
Chapter 4: He Strengthens | 43

PART TWO
THE LAMB OF GOD
Our Source of Covenant Belonging | 52

Chapter 5: He Restores | 55
Chapter 6: He Forgives | 65
Chapter 7: He Delivers and Redeems | 77
Chapter 8: He Covenants | 87

Conclusion: Hosanna and Hallelujah | 95
Notes | 109
Scripture Guide | 121

PREFACE

You and I, we each have a story. A personal story of divine identity and possibilities beyond human imagination—a unique journey to discover, create, grapple with, become.

It is said life can only be understood by looking backward, but it must be lived by looking forward.[1] Often it is in retrospect that we can see God's hand blessing and guiding our lives. Yet sometimes we can also glimpse our eternal journey as a future whole. Sometimes we sense in a moment the heights and depths and all that is between in our faith, hopes, challenges, and covenant promises in the Lord Jesus Christ.

PREFACE

This small book is a story within a story. My part of the story is a meditation on Jesus Christ as the Shepherd and the Lamb. My testimony and reflections draw on the invitation of Jesus Christ, often in His own first-person voice, to understand His love for us as our Good Shepherd and Lamb of God. As we shall see, of the many titles by which Jesus Christ could be known, none is more tender, powerful, or illuminating than the *Shepherd* and the *Lamb*. In this dual, reflexive role—as Shepherd and Lamb—Jesus Christ succors and saves. He lifts and liberates. He rises above and descends below all things.

Your part of the story is also a meditation. If you choose, it can also be an invitation, a call to action. Your part of our shared story is to discover how coming to Jesus Christ as the Shepherd and the Lamb fires your faith, hopes, and spiritual imagination, how it lends perspective to your lived experiences and your faith-filled future. These are the things of our soul we hold in what the poet W. B. Yeats calls our "deep heart's core."[2]

These are the things which connect us and give belonging and meaning with Jesus Christ, those around us, and our truest, best self.

x

PREFACE

Thank you for sharing this story and this reflection together. I hope it brings you closer to Jesus Christ. He is the Light and Life of the World. He is the Father and the Son. He is the Shepherd and the Lamb.

INTRODUCTION

THE SHEPHERD AND THE LAMB

With the shepherd boy who became a king, we declare: "The Lord is my shepherd; I shall not want.

"He maketh me to lie down in green pastures: he leadeth me beside the still waters.

"He restoreth my soul."[1]

At Easter and every day, we celebrate the Good Shepherd who is also the Lamb of God. Of all His divine titles, it is significant that Jesus Christ describes Himself as the Good Shepherd and that prophetic testimonies point us to Him as the Lamb of God. No matter when or where we live, we are drawn to the Shepherd—compassionate, watchful, protecting—and to the Lamb—innocent, forgiving, redeeming.

No matter when or where

we live, we are drawn to the

Shepherd—compassionate,

watchful, protecting—and

to the Lamb—innocent,

forgiving, redeeming.

THE SHEPHERD AND THE LAMB

These symbolic titles are powerfully complementary—who better to succor each precious lamb than the Good Shepherd, and who better to be our Good Shepherd than the Lamb of God?

Jesus Christ testifies, "I am the good shepherd: the good shepherd giveth his life for the sheep."[2] Jesus had power to lay down His life and power to take it up again.[3] Through His Atonement and Resurrection, united with His Father, our Savior uniquely blesses us, relating to us and inviting us to relate to Him and the ways He loves us as both the Good Shepherd and the Lamb of God.

On Easter Sunday, April 3, 1836, the resurrected Jesus Christ came in person to accept the dedication of the Kirtland Temple.[4] Those who saw Him there described Him in complementary contrasts of fire and water: "His eyes were as a flame of *fire*; the hair of his head was white like the pure *snow*; his countenance shone above the brightness of the *sun*; and his voice was as the sound of the *rushing of great waters*, even the voice of Jehovah."[5]

On that occasion, our Savior declared, "I am the first and the last; I am he who liveth, I am he who was slain; I am your advocate with the Father."[6] Again, complementary contrasts—first and last, living and slain. He is Alpha and

THE SHEPHERD AND THE LAMB

Omega, the beginning and the end, the Shepherd and the Lamb.

Jesus Christ is our guide and exemplar as we journey through mortality. He calls us in His name and invites us each to hear His voice and follow Him. He gathers us into His fold with compassion and healing, increasing our faith and capacity to follow in the footsteps of His perfect example. With praise and gratitude, we "press forward with a steadfastness in Christ, having a perfect brightness of hope, and a love of God and of all men [and women]."[7] As we follow Jesus Christ with real intent, we are strengthened in His love. Our desire increases to do justly, love mercy, and walk humbly with God.[8]

Jesus Christ is our perfect Shepherd. We can heed His call and follow His example to "feed [His] lambs."[9] We can become, like Him, shepherds in Israel, ministering to each other in love, as He ministers to us. As we learn to do so, we are strengthened and strengthen each other in His love.

Jesus Christ is the "Lamb of God," the "Son of the Eternal Father, and the Savior of the world."[10] He "taketh away the sin of the world."[11] In vision, Nephi saw the divine mission of the Lamb of God--His being baptized; going forth among the children of men, healing the sick and

4

casting out devils; being judged of the world; and in mercy bringing forth again His plain and precious gospel to all kindreds, tongues, and peoples.[12] With Isaiah, Abinadi testified, "All we, like sheep, have gone astray; we have turned every one to his own way; and the Lord hath laid on him the iniquities of us all."[13] Alma called the great and last sacrifice of Jesus Christ the "one thing which is of more importance than they all."[14] Alma encourages us to "have faith on the Lamb of God" and to "come and fear not."[15]

Jesus Christ calls us in His voice and His name. He seeks, gathers, and comes to His people. Through His living prophet and each of us, He desires all to find peace, purpose, healing, and joy in the fullness of His restored gospel and on His covenant path.

JESUS CHRIST CALLS US IN HIS VOICE AND HIS NAME. HE SEEKS, GATHERS, AND COMES TO HIS PEOPLE.... JESUS CHRIST IS OUR HOPE AND PROMISE FOR ETERNAL SALVATION, OUR SOURCE OF COVENANT BELONGING.

Jesus Christ is our hope and promise for eternal salvation, our source of covenant belonging. He was foreordained before the foundations of the world to be our Deliverer and Redeemer. As the sons and daughters of God shouted for joy at our Eternal Father's plan of happiness,[16] Jesus Christ humbly and meekly said, "Here am I, send me."[17] In time and eternity, Jesus Christ restores that which was lost and should be found. He forgives. He delivers and redeems. He offers covenant belonging, sanctified relationships stronger than the cords of death.

As we become "humble followers of God and the Lamb,"[18] we may have our names written in the Lamb's book of life.[19] We may sing the song of the Lamb.[20] We may be invited to the supper of the Lamb.[21]

As the Shepherd and the Lamb, He calls: come again to "the true knowledge . . . of [your] Redeemer, . . . [your] great and true shepherd."[22]

We shout hosanna and hallelujah!

We praise, "Worthy is the Lamb."[23] "Hosanna to God and the Lamb!"[24]

We remember and rejoice: Jesus Christ is the Good Shepherd, the Lamb of God!

PART ONE

THE GOOD SHEPHERD

*Our Guide
and Exemplar*

The image and symbolism of Jesus Christ as Good Shepherd resonates deep in our souls. I have watched sheep graze in green pastures in New Zealand, a country where sheep outnumber people. I have seen sheep flocks roam amidst the patchwork lemon-lime fields in the Cotswolds of England.[1] I have heard lambs bleating in the Holy Land, where shepherds watched their flocks by night,[2] and where Jesus Christ in His mortal ministry drew us to Himself as our Good Shepherd.

Our Good Shepherd, Jesus Christ calls us in His voice and His name. He seeks and gathers. He ministers in perfect love. He strengthens us in His love and invites us to strengthen each other in Him.

CHAPTER 1

HE CALLS

I have not always loved general conference the way I do now. Of course, general conference means more as, through the years, I gain experience and spiritual maturity. But general conference also means more because those who speak have become my associates, my friends. Almost as soon as they begin speaking, I recognize their voices. I know who is speaking. Their stories and backstories make general conference personal. And in the heartfelt prayers, uplifting music, and inspired messages, I hear through His Spirit the voice of the Good Shepherd.

His is not a voice of fire, thunder, or whirlwind. His is not a harsh voice, nor a loud voice, but it can pierce to our very souls. I am sometimes surprised, though I should not be, that the more we come to know and recognize His voice and Spirit, the softer and quieter they can seem.

Why would a familiar voice feel, in our hearts and minds, quieter rather than louder? Perhaps His voice is not meant to overwhelm us, to press itself upon us. Perhaps, by the very nature of His infinite love, His voice is meant to distill gently upon our souls like the dews from heaven. It is meant to be delicate and refreshing, even while powerful and clear.

All this helps us understand Jesus Christ's declaration that, as our Good Shepherd, He "calleth his own sheep by name. . . . They know his voice."[1] And "in his own name he doth call you, which is the name of Christ."[2]

HIS CALL OFFERS HOPE

I stand all amazed that the Creator of the heavens and the earth knows and calls me by my name, by His voice, in His name. Like our fingerprints, the sound of our voice is individual, distinct, recognizable. So are His voice and name.

We are not meant to wander in existential uncertainty. We can receive His spiritual direction, protection, and inspiration at important times. But we are not meant to be told in every matter how to think or act. Heavenly Father's loving

HE CALLS

plan of happiness includes as a central tenet our God-given agency. For the power is in us to choose and bring to pass righteousness, doing many things by our own choice.[3]

Jesus Christ protects, guides, and watches over us with perfect love. We can become perfect in Him. "Yea, come unto Christ, and be perfected in him . . . , and love God with all your might, mind and strength, then is his grace sufficient for you, that by his grace ye may be perfect in Christ."[4]

Our Shepherd calls us in His voice and name with love and possibility. He invites us to know by our own experience the good way, the liberating truth, the abundant life.[5] To those who feel burdened, He invites, "Come unto me," and to those who come to Him, He promises, "I will give you rest."[6]

We look forward with faith and trust in our Good Shepherd when things do not go as we hope, expect, or perhaps deserve. There may be no fault of ours. We may have done our best. Yet, in various times and ways, we all feel inadequate, uncertain, perhaps unworthy. Along life's path, we may lose faith in the Good Shepherd, but He never loses faith in us. As it were, God's porch light is always on. It is said, however we may hide, we want to be found. Though we may turn our face from Him, He never loses sight of us. Always, He invites us to come or return to the covenants that mark

13

It is said, however we may hide, we want
to be found. Though we may turn our
face from Him, He never loses sight of us.
Always, He invites us to come or return
to the covenants that mark His path. He
waits ready to embrace us, even when we
wander and are "yet a great way off."

His path. He waits ready to embrace us, even when we wander and are "yet a great way off."[7] His heart is with the ninety-and-nine, even as He calls to the one.

When we look with an eye of faith for the patterns, arc, or connected dots of our experience, we can see His tender mercies and encouragement, especially in our trials, sorrows, and challenges, but also in our joys. However often we stumble or fall, if we keep moving toward Him, He will help us, a step at a time.

Our Good Shepherd knows when we feel alone, diminished, uncertain, or afraid. Are you the only member of the Church in your family, school, workplace, or community? Does your branch sometimes feel small or isolated? Have you moved to a new place, perhaps with an unfamiliar language or customs? Perhaps your life's circumstances have changed, and things you never thought possible now confront you? Whoever we are, whatever our challenges, hopes, and dreams, our promise is that we can receive "true knowledge . . . of [our] Redeemer, [our] great and true shepherd, and be numbered among his sheep."[8]

We hearken to the call of our Good Shepherd as we follow His perfect, obedient example. As we do so, inspiration comes to do good, to love God, and to serve Him.[9] As we

THE SHEPHERD AND THE LAMB

study, ponder, and pray; as we regularly make anew sacramental and temple covenants; and as we invite all to come to His gospel and ordinances, we are hearkening to His voice.

IN HIS NAME

Jesus Christ calls us to His restored Church, called by His name, The Church of Jesus Christ of Latter-day Saints. He explains, "And how be it my church save it be called in my name? For if a church be called in Moses' name then it be Moses' church; or if it be called in the name of a man then it be the church of a man; but if it be called *in my name* then it is my church, if it so be that they are built upon my gospel."[10] Of course, Jesus Christ represents both form and substance. His restored Church is called in His name. It is built upon His gospel.

Jesus Christ continues, "Therefore, whatsoever ye shall do, ye shall do it *in my name;* therefore ye shall call the church *in my name;* and ye shall call upon the Father *in my name* that he will bless the church for my sake." And then comes this glorious promise: "Therefore if ye call upon the Father, for the church, if it be *in my name* the Father will hear you."[11]

Jesus Christ calls us in His voice and name to come unto Him. He calls us to serve and to consecrate what we do in His name. As we serve those around us as He would, we draw closer to Him. In a small way, we understand and become more like Him as we do what He would do, as He would do it. He calls us to draw unto Him as we change and repent; His sanctifying Atonement can truly help us become more compassionate, more selfless, more holy. He calls us to take upon us His holy name through sacred ordinances and covenants, connecting us to God and each other in time and eternity.

Our Shepherd is Himself the gate, the door, the strait and narrow covenant path for His sheep.[12]

Our Good Shepherd invites us to lie down in verdant green pastures;[13] to "buy milk and honey, without money and without price;"[14] to find His abundant and eternal life.[15] Exaltation is to know God, that where He is we "shall be also." And eternal life is "to know the only wise and true God, and Jesus Christ, whom he hath sent."[16] As both the Shepherd and the Lamb,

As our Good Shepherd, His call is constant and sure, compassionate and kind, still and piercing to the heart. He never gives up on us. He invites us not to give up on each other.

THE SHEPHERD AND THE LAMB

Jesus Christ exemplifies the truth that "he that exalteth himself shall be abased, and he that abaseth himself shall be exalted."[17]

As our Good Shepherd, His call is constant and sure, compassionate and kind, still and piercing to the heart. He never gives up on us. He invites us not to give up on each other. Jesus Christ honors our agency even as He beckons us to come unto Him, whatever our state of mind, faith, or heart.

His is a Shepherd's heart. His is a Shepherd's call. His are a Shepherd's voice and name—to the world and to you and me—each of us.

CHAPTER 2

HE GATHERS

In every time and place, the Good Shepherd "shall gather the lambs with his arm, and carry them in his bosom, and shall gently lead those that are with young."[1] Jesus Christ gathers the scattered house of Israel into His single fold.[2] His gathering reaches to every geography, every person, every historical age and circumstance. He invites all nations, kindreds, tongues, and people "to come unto him and partake of his goodness; . . . black and white, bond and free, male and female; . . . all are alike unto God."[3] Like His Atonement, the gathering of His covenant people is infinite and eternal, at once breathtakingly universal in its scope and breathtakingly personal in its invitation.

Like His Atonement, the gathering of His covenant people is infinite and eternal, at once breathtakingly universal in its scope and breathtakingly personal in its invitation.

HE GATHERS

Jesus Christ, the Shepherd of Israel, gathers His people in all places and circumstances into the safety of His fold on both sides of the veil.

GATHERING INTO HIS ONE FOLD

Our Good Shepherd seeks and gathers us. He asks, "What man of you, having an hundred sheep, if he lose one of them, doth not leave the ninety and nine in the wilderness, and go after that which is lost, *until he find it*?"[4]

Our Shepherd reaches out to us in all our varied circumstances. He acknowledges the ninety-nine who are steadfast and immovable, even while He yearns after the one who has strayed. Our Shepherd seeks and delivers us, individually and collectively, "out of all places,"[5] "from the four quarters of the earth."[6] He gathers us by holy covenant and His atoning blood.[7]

The Good Shepherd speaks with clarity and compassion about all His sheep. "I am the good shepherd, and know my sheep, and am known of mine. As the Father knoweth me, even so know I the Father: and I lay down my life for the sheep."[8]

As He told His New Testament disciples, the Good Shepherd has "other sheep . . . which are not of this fold." He

23

declares that "them also I must bring, and they shall hear my voice; and there shall be one fold, and one shepherd."[9] In the Book of Mormon, the resurrected Good Shepherd testified to Lehi's covenant children, "Ye are my sheep."[10] And Jesus said there are yet other sheep who would hear His voice.[11] His prophetic words are being fulfilled as His restored gospel continues to spread among every nation, kindred, and tongue.

As the Good Shepherd, Jesus Christ knows each sheep, each lamb. He promises His Father not one given Him will be lost. Speaking of His disciples, Jesus Christ tells His Father, "While I was with them in the world, I kept them in thy name: those that thou gavest me I have kept, and none of them is lost."[12] Each is remembered; none is forgotten.

Similarly, in our latter days, the Good Shepherd reiterates, "Fear not, little children, for you are mine, and I have overcome the world, and you are of them that my Father hath given me; and none of them that my Father hath given me shall be lost. . . . Wherefore, I am in your midst, and I am the good shepherd."[13] In this life, we or those we love may wander for a season, but we and they are never lost to the Good Shepherd.

HE GATHERS IN COMPASSION

Our Good Shepherd gathers us by understanding everything in our human, mortal condition. As the sacrificial Lamb of God, Jesus Christ "suffer[ed] pains and afflictions and temptations of every kind." Jesus Christ has taken upon Himself our infirmities. He experienced "the pains and the sicknesses of his people . . . , that his bowels may be filled with mercy, according to the flesh." As Shepherd and Lamb, Jesus Christ knows "how to succor his people" and can "blot out their transgressions according to the power of his deliverance."[14]

As prophecies foretold, Jesus Christ was lifted up to lift us all to Him. He "suffered these things for all, that [we] might not suffer if [we] would repent." This suffering caused Him, "even God, the greatest of all, to tremble because of pain, and to bleed at every pore." He suffered "body and spirit." He pleaded not to drink the bitter cup. Nevertheless, glorying the Father, He did not shrink but "partook and finished [His] preparations unto the children of men."[15]

> AS THE GOOD SHEPHERD, JESUS CHRIST KNOWS EACH SHEEP, EACH LAMB. HE PROMISES HIS FATHER NOT ONE GIVEN HIM WILL BE LOST.

Heartfelt feeling often transcends words. Our Shepherd gathers us when we have no words or way to express what we feel. Thus, "the Spirit also helpeth our infirmities: for we know not what we should pray for as we ought: but the Spirit itself maketh intercession for us with groanings [*sighings* in the Greek] which cannot be uttered."[16] Nor were there words when the Nephites witnessed Jesus Christ ministering to them: "No tongue can speak, neither can there be written by any man, neither can the hearts of men conceive so great and marvelous things as we both saw and heard Jesus speak; and no one can conceive of the joy which filled our souls at the time we heard him pray for us unto the Father."[17]

Scriptural verses record Jesus Christ's tenderness and compassion. When His joy was full, Jesus Christ wept. "And the multitude bare record of it, and he took their little children, one by one, and blessed them, and prayed unto the Father for them. And when he had done this he wept again."[18]

Sometimes we apologize when we weep—even when our tears come forth in spontaneous joy or unmitigated sorrow. In all things, Jesus Christ is our perfect example. In joy and sorrow, He weeps with us. In joy and sorrow, He weeps for us.

To be the Shepherd is to weep with joy and compassion.

HE GATHERS

He invites us to weep too, with more joy in Him and more compassion for others.

GATHERING THROUGH TEMPLE COVENANTS

Our Good Shepherd, Jesus Christ gathers us by covenant into the garners of the house of the Lord.[19]

In the early days of the Restoration, as the latter-day gathering commenced, Jesus Christ and the great prophets of old, Moses, Elias, and Elijah, came to restore priesthood keys and authority. Thus, "the keys of this dispensation are committed"[20] within Jesus Christ's restored Church to bless all God's children.

The coming of Elijah in the Kirtland Temple also fulfilled Malachi's Old Testament prophecy that Elijah would return as part of the gathering of the roots and branches of Israel "before the coming of the great and dreadful day of the Lord."[21] In doing so, Elijah's appearance coincided, not by coincidence, with the Jewish Passover season, which tradition reverently anticipates Elijah's return.

Many devout Jewish families set a place for Elijah at their Passover table. Many fill a cup to the brim to invite and welcome him. And some, during the traditional Passover seder, send a child to the door, sometimes left partly open, to see if Elijah is outside, waiting to be invited in.[22]

27

In fulfillment of prophecy and as part of the promised "restoration of all things,"[23] Elijah did come as promised, at Easter and the onset of Passover. He brought the sealing authority to bind families on earth and in heaven. As Moroni taught the Prophet Joseph, Elijah "shall plant in the hearts of the children the promises made to the fathers, and the hearts of the children shall turn to their fathers." "If it were not so," Moroni continued, "the whole earth would be utterly wasted at [the Lord's] coming."[24] The spirit of Elijah, a manifestation of the Holy Ghost bearing witness of eternal family, helps gather us in our generations. This help includes inspiring us in our genealogy, family history, and sacred temple service.

Said the Prophet Joseph Smith: "It may seem to some to be a very bold doctrine that we talk of—a power which records or binds on earth and binds in heaven. Nevertheless, in all ages of the world, whenever the Lord has given a dispensation of the priesthood to any man by actual revelation, or any set of men, this power has always been given."[25]

And so it is today. Sacred covenants and ordinances, not available anywhere else, but coming to more places than ever before, draw us closer to God our Father and Jesus Christ in the holy house of the Lord. Promised blessings come through restored priesthood keys, doctrine, and authority. They reflect our faith, obedience, and the promises of His Holy Spirit to us in our generations, in time and eternity.

Through Jesus Christ's Atonement and the power of covenants made in His holy name with God, our Eternal Father, we can be happy and forever with our loved ones and the Good Shepherd. As children we believed in the archetypal promise that we can live happily ever after. In Jesus Christ, it is true. We are meant to be gathered in joy for eternity. Thankfully, Jesus Christ's Atonement overcomes physical death. And Jesus Christ's Atonement helps us change, repent, and become better, sanctified, even perfect in Him.[26] Especially when we make each other unhappy or are unkind or are trapped in a past filled with abuse or indifference or lack of concern, if we choose to follow Him, His can be a liberating path forward to peace, healing, and reconciliation.

Glory be to God! Our Good Shepherd gathers us and provides a way, in time and eternity, that we can be happy and forever with Him and those we love.

CHAPTER 3

HE MINISTERS

Jesus Christ ministers. He ministers perfectly by His very nature because of who He is. Because He is good, He can go about doing good.[1] We become more like the Good Shepherd when we minister "unto . . . the least of these" as we would unto Him;[2] when we love our neighbor as ourselves;[3] when we "love one another" as He loves us;[4] and when we appreciate that "whosoever will be great among you, let him be your minister."[5]

When Jesus Christ called Saul (who became the Apostle Paul), the Lord said, "Stand upon thy feet: for I have appeared unto thee for this purpose, to make thee a minister and a witness."[6] To minister as the Good Shepherd would is

THE SHEPHERD AND THE LAMB

to be a witness of Jesus Christ. To be a witness of Jesus Christ is to minister as the Good Shepherd would have us do.

HOW THE GOOD SHEPHERD MINISTERS

Our Good Shepherd ministers with pure love. The scriptures movingly describe Jesus Christ's compassion when He meets the sick, afflicted, and despondent; when He restores to life the only son of a destitute, grieving widow;[7] when He meets multitudes "scattered abroad, as sheep having no shepherd."[8] He feeds the multitudes who have been with Him three days, whom He fears may faint with hunger. He gives thanks, blesses, breaks, and miraculously makes five loaves and three small fishes sufficient for all to eat and be filled.[9] Even on His way to raise the little (only) daughter of a synagogue ruler, Jesus Christ stops to minister to the one.[10] In the bustle and push of the crowd, He feels virtue heal a woman who with faith has touched His garment hem. Beset twelve years by a flow of blood, she had spent all her living upon physicians, with "nothing bettered, but rather grew worse."[11] But, with His blessing, He assures her, "Daughter, be of good comfort: thy faith hath made thee whole."[12]

At the beginning of His mortal ministry, Jesus Christ

calls twelve disciples. He ministers to them in terms they know—catching fish. At His word, after toiling all night without catching any fish, they again cast and catch so many fish that their nets break.[13] At the conclusion of Jesus Christ's mortal ministry, His disciples again fish all night without success. At His word, they cast once more, this time on the other side of the ship. As before, their nets overflow with fish, but this time—symbolically—their nets do not break.[14]

Because the Good Shepherd is always concerned for the one and the ninety-nine, He constantly ministers to both—serving and teaching the individual one and ninety-nine at the same time. This principle of simultaneously blessing the one and the ninety-nine is illustrated throughout scripture. Scripture addresses the needs and questions of specific individuals who live in specific times and circumstances. At the same time, God's revelations and instructions found in scripture apply to and bless people in every time and place.

Section 11 of the Doctrine and Covenants provides an example. This section records revelation the Prophet Joseph Smith received to address the questions of his brother Hyrum Smith, who desired to prepare and qualify for missionary service. Though this revealed guidance and wisdom was addressed to a single individual (Hyrum Smith) at a specific time and place (May 1829 in Harmony, Pennsylvania), these plain and precious truths bless all preparing for missions.[15] All who read, study, and ponder these revealed passages now hear the Lord's instructions:

"A great and marvelous work is about to come forth among the children of men."[16]

"Whoso desireth to reap let him thrust in his sickle with his might, and reap while the day lasts, that he may treasure up for his soul everlasting salvation in the kingdom of God."[17]

"Whosoever will thrust in his sickle and reap, the same is called of God."[18]

"Put your trust in that Spirit which leadeth to do good—yea, to do justly, to walk humbly, to judge righteously; and this is my Spirit."[19]

And, as missionaries in the Missionary Training Center (MTC) learn: "Seek not to declare my word, but first seek to obtain my word, and then shall your tongue be loosed; then, if you desire, you shall have my Spirit and my word, yea, the power of God unto the convincing of men."[20]

We find instruction, guidance, and inspiration in each section of the Doctrine of Covenants as our Good Shepherd often ministers to the one and ninety-nine at the same time.

OUR CALL TO FEED HIS SHEEP

As the "Shepherd of Israel,"[21] Jesus Christ exemplifies how shepherds in Israel minister in love. Good shepherds strengthen, heal, bind up that which is broken. They bring again that which was driven away. They seek that which was lost.[22] Good shepherds reach out, understand others where they are, and build gospel fellowship, including by regularly visiting, sharing, and inviting each other in our homes and neighborhoods.

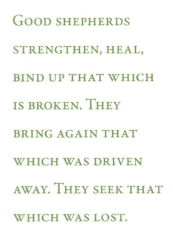

> GOOD SHEPHERDS STRENGTHEN, HEAL, BIND UP THAT WHICH IS BROKEN. THEY BRING AGAIN THAT WHICH WAS DRIVEN AWAY. THEY SEEK THAT WHICH WAS LOST.

Good shepherds love and, when appropriate, extend inspired invitations. Inspired invitations help us better make and keep sacred covenants. They help us become more kind, considerate, and helpful with each other. They help us become more humble and open, less like a natural man or woman and more like a child. They help us trust and forgive more, judge and criticize less. Inspired invitations given in His ministering love change lives.

Our Good Shepherd also has words of warning for us as we prepare to minister as shepherds in Israel. He cautions

Good shepherds . . . help us become more kind, considerate, and helpful with each other. They help us become more humble and open, less like a natural man or woman and more like a child. They help us trust and forgive more, judge and criticize less.

HE MINISTERS

that shepherds in Israel must not slumber.[23] We must take care not to scatter or cause the sheep to go astray.[24] We are to act with true charity, and not look our own way for our own gain.[25]

The Lord also warns of hirelings, who "careth not for the sheep,"[26] and "false prophets, who come to you in sheep's clothing, but inwardly they are ravening wolves."[27] Likewise, as we minister, we are to do so as our Savior would and never hurt, deceive, or lead astray. Our Good Shepherd is our example. He calls and takes care of His sheep by name. They know His name and voice—that of Jesus Christ.[28]

There are needs everywhere in today's world. Good shepherds, good neighbors, seek to do good in the name of Jesus Christ among God's children everywhere. We can each do more by working together. Through significant humanitarian efforts, His restored Church strives to serve scores of countries and hundreds of communities. Clean water, sanitation, literacy, women's safety and shelters, mobility devices such as wheelchairs and walkers, infant resuscitation, self-reliance, addiction recovery, food security—the list of the Church's humanitarian service goes on.

Of course, no group or institution can do everything needed. Service in Him also occurs, one on one, through the

37

dedicated, often unspoken, efforts of thousands of individual Church members reaching out to those around them. I am grateful that so many brothers and sisters who are members of The Church of Jesus Christ of Latter-day Saints minister in their wards and branches and in their communities as volunteers, motivated by the pure love and charity of our Good Shepherd.

Higher and holier ministering[29] comes when we pray for "the pure love of Christ"[30] and follow the Spirit. Everywhere I am inspired by those who love and minister as the Good Shepherd would. Here is an example:

When I met Jeff and his wife, Melissa, they were attending general conference for his first time. Melissa is a lifelong Church member and returned missionary. Jeff is a former professional baseball player (he was a catcher) and now a physician anesthesiologist. This couple had met, fallen in love, married, and been blessed with a beautiful daughter. Not a member of the Church, Jeff had come to general conference wondering if Jesus Christ's gospel and church had been restored, including with apostles and prophets. He told me, "Much to my surprise, I am moving toward baptism because it feels like the most authentic and honest way to live."

Earlier, as Jeff had been learning about the restored

gospel at his local church congregation, he had been assigned a ministering brother. However, Melissa had apologetically warned Jeff's assigned ministering brother, "Jeff does not want 'white shirts' in our house." So Jeff's assigned ministering brother found comfortable ways for Jeff and him to talk and do things together. He and Jeff became good friends.

Not surprisingly, ministering in a gospel way to Jeff also blessed and strengthened his ministering brother. The ministering brother also found gospel joy, peace, and testimony in Jesus Christ as he ministered as the Good Shepherd would.

MINISTERING NURTURES SPIRITUAL COMMUNITY

Inspired ministering blesses families and individuals; it also strengthens gospel community in wards and branches. Think of your ward or branch as a spiritual community, a spiritual ecosystem. In the Book of Mormon allegory of the olive trees, the Lord of the vineyard and His servants bring forth precious fruit. They strengthen each tree by binding together the strengths and weaknesses of all the trees.[31] The Lord of the vineyard and His servants repeatedly ask, "What more can I do?"[32] Together, we can bless hearts and homes, wards and branches, through inspired, consistent ministering.[33]

Ministering—shepherding—makes our vineyard "one body"[34]—a sacred grove. Each tree in our grove is a living family tree. Roots and branches intertwine. Ministering blesses generations. There is something very precious in established gospel communities, in caring stakes and wards, in supportive districts and branches. Gospel patterns include multiple generations nourishing each other. Parents nourish children who become parents who nourish their children, as parents become grandparents and great-grandparents who continue to nurture children and grandchildren. This process of righteous generations being welded together in love by covenant is central to God's purpose and loving plan of happiness.

While we may tire physically, in His service we do "not weary in well-doing."[35] We diligently do our best without running faster than we have strength.[36] We trust that "God loveth a cheerful giver."[37] For God, who "ministereth seed to the sower," will "both minister bread for your food, and multiply your seed sown."[38] In other words, God enriches "every thing to all bountifulness."[39] They "which soweth bountifully shall reap also bountifully."[40]

HE MINISTERS

Wherever we are, let us reach out and care as our Good Shepherd would. In our efforts to minister as our Good Shepherd does, may we draw closer to Jesus Christ and each other, becoming more like Jesus Christ and the followers of the Good Shepherd He would have us be.

CHAPTER 4

HE STRENGTHENS

Our guide and exemplar, the Good Shepherd strengthens us on the strait and narrow path which leads to eternal life.[1] Following His path—the covenant path—strengthens us in our Savior's love and teaches us to strengthen each other as He would.

The Good Shepherd knows us perfectly. "God is not mocked,"[2] nor can He be deceived. With full knowledge of who we are and all we have done, He can in mercy and justice encircle the humble and penitent in His arms of safety.

In the Kirtland Temple, the Prophet Joseph Smith saw in vision his brother Alvin saved in the celestial kingdom. Joseph marveled since Alvin had died before receiving the

THE SHEPHERD AND THE LAMB

saving ordinance of baptism.[3] Comfortingly, the Lord explained why: the Lord "will judge [us] according to [our] works, according to the desire of [our] hearts."[4] Our souls—our spirits and physical bodies—bear record of our works and desires.

WAITING UPON THE LORD

Some years ago, it was my privilege to perform the temple marriage of an older couple. Then seventy years old, the bride had waited all her life to be married and sealed in the house of the Lord. Now it was her day. She shyly swished her beautiful wedding dress, this way, then that way. She radiated gospel beauty. (Of course, Sister Gong is *the* most beautiful bride I have ever seen.) I humbly thought, "The Lord keeps His promises." Some are fulfilled earlier, some later, but in His time and way, He fulfills His promises.

Speaking words given him by an angel, King Benjamin underscores our Good Shepherd's promise to those who wait faithfully upon the Lord: "For behold, they are blessed in all things, both temporal and spiritual; and if they hold out faithful to the end they are received into heaven, that thereby they may dwell with God in a state of never-ending happiness."[5]

44

HE STRENGTHENS

These promises offer hope and assurance when blessings we may righteously desire do not come at the time or in the way we may earnestly pray. Waiting upon the Lord is a sacred position. Said the Psalmist, "Those that wait upon the Lord, they shall inherit the earth."[6]

A friend who had already battled cancer was later severely injured when a car hit him while he was walking. Lying in the hospital in pain, he reflected on what he could learn from his situation. He wondered if he would walk again. Waiting day after day upon the Lord made Isaiah's promise meaningful and real for him: "They that wait upon the Lord shall renew their strength; they shall mount up with wings as eagles; they shall run, and not be weary; and they shall walk, and not faint."[7]

Our Shepherd knows. He cares. He is with us.

OUR SHEPHERD'S WATCH-CARE

In specifically individual and personal ways, our Good Shepherd's infinite love, eternal wisdom, and divine power bless us. Tender and wise, Jesus Christ blesses us best and most. With infinite compassion, He knows all the beginnings and all the ends.

He strengthens us in His love when we feel alone and

Our Good Shepherd's infinite love,

eternal wisdom, and divine power

bless us. Tender and wise, Jesus

Christ blesses us best and most. With

infinite compassion, He knows all the

beginnings and all the ends.

misunderstood. The only member of the Church in her family, a dear young woman was uncertain about God's love for her. Those around her laughed at and made fun of her. An inspired priesthood blessing helped her feel her divine worth as a beloved daughter of God, a child of the covenant.

A son grew up not knowing his father, who had been killed when the son was very young. Now this courageous young man seeks to learn about his father by meeting those who knew his father, who he was and what he was like. Life has sometimes been hard without a father nearby, but this young man finds strength in the love of those around him and the Lord.

Patriarchal blessings strengthen us through spiritual covenant connection. This is not surprising. Patriarchal blessings declare our spiritual lineage in the house of Israel. They personalize for us the promises given Abraham, Isaac, and Jacob—the great patriarchs of old who received covenant promises from the Lord. Those promises bless us each as children of the covenant.

I have deep love for the patriarchs of the Church. My father was a patriarch. My brother is a patriarch. When I visit a stake, I feel it a great privilege to visit with the patriarch and his wife. I am always deeply moved by the humility and preparation our patriarchs exemplify as they spiritually connect those receiving their blessing with the Lord.

Patriarchs know Heavenly Father's intimate knowledge of and love for each of His children. A stake president told me he wanted his son to receive a patriarchal blessing from his stake's older, more experienced patriarch, but it did not work out that way. "As the recently called patriarch gave my son his patriarchal blessing," the stake president said, "phrases from my own patriarchal blessing were spoken. It was as though the Lord was gently reminding me He, not the patriarch, is the source of inspiration for patriarchal blessings."

How grateful we are that patriarchal blessings and other blessings strengthen us with unmistakable assurance that we belong by covenant to God and with each other.

OUR TRUE, DIVINE SELVES

We find our true, divine selves when we follow our Good Shepherd and come to God our Father by covenant. We receive strength and perspective when, in Alma's words, we enter "into a covenant with [the Lord], that [we] will serve him and keep his commandments, that he may pour out his Spirit more abundantly upon [us]."[8] When we want to change for the better—as one friend put it, when we want "to stop being miserable and to be happy being happy"—we become open to direction, help, and strength. When we belong by covenant with God and a community of faithful believers, we can receive the blessings promised in the doctrine of Christ.[9] This process can begin today.

This world is full of mirage, illusion, sleight of hand. So much seems transitory and superficial. When we put aside the masks, pretense, crowd-sourced likes and dislikes, we yearn for more than fleeting veneer, ephemeral connection, or the pursuit of worldly self-interest. Gratefully, there is a way to find answers that matter.

When we come to God's great commandments to love Him and those around us, we do so not as a stranger or guest but as His child at home.[10] Everything changes when we, as children of the covenant, know His promises bless us now. These covenant promises offer hope and assurance today, and beyond time into eternity.

Understanding our divine identity can profoundly change even our

EVERYTHING CHANGES WHEN WE, AS CHILDREN OF THE COVENANT, KNOW HIS PROMISES BLESS US NOW. THESE COVENANT PROMISES OFFER HOPE AND ASSURANCE TODAY, AND BEYOND TIME INTO ETERNITY.

most entrenched behavior. Profound change in how we act is often preceded by understanding who we are. A man I met in Central America told me he had lived aimlessly on the street until he was taught the truths of the gospel of Jesus Christ and his identity as a child of God. These truths changed his life and those of his family members. He found purpose, motivation, and focus. He began working hard and smart. Today he blesses many through his professional and Church service.

> IN LOSING OUR WORLDLY SELF IN THE STRENGTH OF OUR GOOD SHEPHERD, WE FIND AND BECOME OUR BEST ETERNAL SELF — FREE, ALIVE, REAL.

The age-old paradox is still true. In losing our worldly self in the strength of our Good Shepherd, we find and become our best eternal self[11]—free, alive, real. We redefine our most important and cherished relationships. As we make and keep solemn covenant promises, we invite the power of godliness to be manifest in our lives.[12] When we find strength in Jesus Christ, we can become more than we are. Coming to our Good Shepherd gives us place, narrative, and capacity to become. It produces faith unto life and salvation.[13]

Through His Atonement, we find faith, strength, and

trust to come unto Jesus Christ, knowing perfection is in Him. This knowledge offers an escape from the always-anxious treadmill of perfectionism. It helps us let go of self-imposed worldly expectations that never satisfy. It helps us hold on to every good thing that our Good Shepherd offers.

As we discover our true, divine selves in Jesus Christ, we also learn to recognize and love our brothers and sisters as eternal beings with divine potential. This deepening love and knowledge invites, empowers, and sanctifies us to know and, in our own way, to become more like Him.

PART TWO

THE LAMB
OF GOD

Our Source of

Covenant Belonging

Jesus Christ was prepared from the foundation of the earth as the sacrificial Lamb of God. Meek and lowly, He was innocent, guiltless, without sin. At the same time, full of majesty and power, He was capable and commissioned to overcome death and sin, to make right sorrow, injustice, unfairness, and hard-heartedness. Infinite and eternal, His Atonement is central to the plan of happiness and the purpose of creation.

In all He does, the Lamb of God assures us that He carries us next to His heart. He restores. He forgives. He delivers and redeems. He covenants to give us belonging with God and each other—belonging that sanctifies life and transcends death.

CHAPTER 5

HE RESTORES

As our Shepherd, Jesus Christ protects and watches over us; as the Lamb of God, His atoning sacrifice restores. Significantly, the "power and resurrection of Christ"[1] is manifest in two restorations—physical and spiritual. We commemorate and celebrate Jesus Christ's Resurrection at Easter, but the restorations He wrought through His Resurrection and Atonement bless us every day.

PHYSICAL RESTORATION

Physical resurrection includes restoration of our "proper and perfect frame"; "every limb and joint" will be restored; and "even a hair of the head shall not be lost."[2] This promise gives hope to those who have lost limbs; cannot see, hear, or

THE SHEPHERD AND THE LAMB

walk; feel lost to relentless disease, mental illness, or other diminished capacity. He finds us. He makes us physically whole and complete. He makes us holy.

Aging is a natural part of mortality. Our bodies and minds get older, typically, over time, becoming less able and more frail. Of course we gain in experience and wisdom what we may gradually lose in physical flexibility or mental acumen. We would not trade what we have learned for how we have learned it.

It seems quite purposeful that we begin and end our lives physically dependent on others. As a baby we are dependent on those around us. Similarly, as life concludes, we are often again dependent on others. In between we have opportunity to care for those both younger and older, and those more dependent, than we. Parents who love and care for their children when the children are young often receive the harvest of those early years when the parents later become dependent on their children. In a sense, this is a pattern in which now-older sheep care for those who once tended them as lambs.

Jesus Christ, the Lamb of God, promises us each physical restoration. This promise flows from two realities of creation: first, our soul unites an eternal spirit and a physical body for the duration of motality; and second, our spirit and body

HE RESTORES

receive a fullness of joy only when inseparably reunited following the Resurrection. Death and resurrection are central to God's eternal plan of happiness. The sacrifice of the Lamb of God makes possible the gift of universal resurrection. "For as in Adam all die, even so in Christ shall all be made alive."[3] Alive in Jesus Christ includes immortality—His gift of our physical resurrection. But physical restoration is incomplete unless it also includes a spiritual restoration.

SPIRITUAL RESTORATION

The second restoration is spiritual. "All things shall be restored to their proper order."[4] This spiritual restoration of things to their proper order reflects our works and desires. Jesus Christ restores "that which is good," "righteous," "just," and "merciful."[5]

No wonder the prophet Alma uses the word *restore* twenty-two times[6] as he urges us to be "merciful unto [our] brethren [and sisters]; deal justly, judge righteously, and do good continually." Alma teaches: "And if ye do all these things then shall ye receive your reward; yea, ye shall have mercy *restored* unto you again; ye shall have justice *restored* unto you again; ye shall have a righteous judgment *restored* unto you again; and ye shall have good rewarded unto you again. For that which ye do send out shall return unto you again, and be *restored*."[7]

Jesus Christ promises not simply to
restore what was, but what should be.
Through His every good gift and grace,
we can look forward to the restoration
and restitution of what a loving,
almighty God would wish us to have.

HE RESTORES

This spiritual restoration is bread upon the waters.[8] It is made possible through the Atonement of the Lamb of God. Indeed, "God himself atoneth for the sins of the world."[9] Jesus Christ knows our pains, afflictions, sicknesses, our "temptations of every kind."[10] He can, with mercy, succor us according to our infirmities.[11] Because God is "a perfect, just God, and a merciful God also," the plan of mercy can "appease the demands of justice."[12] We repent and do all we can, and He encircles us "eternally in the arms of his love."[13]

Part of the miracle of spiritual restoration is that Jesus Christ promises to bring back not only what was but also what can and should be. So much of mortal life is disorderly, seemingly unjust and unfair. The natural, physical order of a fallen world, along with the consequences of human myopia, imperfection, callousness, selfishness, and greed, can lead to chronic hunger, disease, trauma, abuse, violence, exploitation, degrading treatment, and challenging circumstances.

Jesus Christ promises not simply to restore what was, but what should be. Through His every good gift and grace, we can look forward to the restoration and restitution of what a loving, almighty God would wish us to have.

Restoration and restitution can begin in this life as we,

with faith and hope in Jesus Christ, make peace with each other and rise above our circumstances.

I remember traveling with a priesthood leader in a distant country that had suffered the atrocities of war. As we passed a certain bend in the river, he said, "When I was in school, soldiers came and tied the hands of my classmates behind their backs and threw them into the river to drown." Miraculously, he was spared. "For a long time," he said, "life had no purpose, meaning, or justice."

He continued, "One night many years later, I saw in a dream one of my classmates who had been drowned. He was wearing a white shirt and black pants. He was smiling. I wondered how he could be smiling and at peace. He was holding what I later understood was a sacrament tray, a symbol of sacred ordinances and covenants. He told me I could find meaning and peace in the restored gospel of Jesus Christ. I have found His peace and purpose in my life."

Even in the worst of circumstances, things beyond anything we can imagine or would want ever to recall, we can remember the Lamb of God and the price and debt He has paid for us.

Sometimes only possible through Jesus Christ, forgiveness liberates. Sometimes only possible in Jesus Christ, hope

Sometimes only possible

through Jesus Christ, forgiveness

liberates. Sometimes only

possible in Jesus Christ, hope

frees us from the past to

have a future.

frees us from the past to have a future. This world is full of injustice, iniquity, inequity, unfairness, and hurt. "Be not overcome of evil, but overcome evil with good"[14] is Jesus Christ's admonition to each of us. In some way, we have all been wronged, insulted, ignored, battered, or traumatized—and, in some way, we have all hurt, misused, neglected others, whether deliberately or unintentionally. Saith the Lord, "Recompense to no man evil for evil"; "avenge not yourselves . . . for it is written, Vengeance is mine; I will repay."[15]

As One who knows, the Lamb of God gently entreats us, "Rejoice with them that do rejoice, and weep with them that weep."[16] Our good on its own is never sufficient to overcome the world; nor have we reason on our own to be of good cheer. That is why we trust and express gratitude that the Lamb of God promises, "In the world ye shall have tribulation: but be of good cheer; I have overcome the world."[17]

These promises are for not only a future life. They are for us here and now. Jesus Christ lives and loves us. He calls and comes to us today. When there is so much hurt and challenge in mortality, Jesus Christ invites us to minister good—to clothe the naked, feed the hungry, liberate the captive, and administer relief to the sick and the afflicted.[18]

Spoken, always, like a Shepherd and a Lamb.

CHAPTER 6

HE FORGIVES

Sometimes we feel distant from Jesus Christ. We say He is the Lamb of God but may not feel or want His watchcare or understand His sacrifice for us.

The Apostle Paul asks, "Who shall separate us from the love of Christ?" He answers, "Neither death, nor life, . . . nor height, nor depth, . . . shall be able to separate us from the love of God, which is in Christ Jesus our Lord."[1] Yet, there is someone who can separate us from God and Jesus Christ—and that someone is us, ourselves. As Isaiah says, "Your sins have hid his face from you."[2]

By divine love and divine law, we are responsible for our choices and their consequences. But our Savior's atoning love

THE SHEPHERD AND THE LAMB

is "infinite and eternal."[3] Whenever we are ready to come home, God is reaching out with great compassion to welcome us, joyfully offering all He is.[4]

President J. Reuben Clark taught: "I believe that our Heavenly Father wants to save every one of his children[,] . . . that in his justice and mercy he will give us the maximum reward for our acts, give us all that he can give, and in the reverse, I believe that he will impose upon us the minimum penalty which it is possible for him to impose."[5]

President Russell M. Nelson invites us to experience the joy of repentance—of doing all we can—so we can receive the forgiveness and blessings Jesus Christ offers. This is possible as we "change the way we love, think, serve, spend our time, treat our wives [and husbands], teach our children, and even care for our bodies."[6]

Scripture teaches that we are saved by Jesus Christ and His grace, "after all we can do."[7] On the cross, even our Savior's merciful plea to His Father was not unconditional. He did not say, "Father, forgive them." Rather, He said, "Father, forgive them; for they know not what they do."[8] We are accountable before God and ourselves for who we are, for what we think, know, and do. Thankfully, we can trust Jesus Christ, the Lamb of God, to judge perfectly and mercifully our intents and actions, as we come to Him with faith and repentance.

CHRIST'S PERFECT LOVE

A dear friend shared how she gained a personal testimony of the Atonement of Jesus Christ and the forgiveness it makes possible. Growing up, she always wondered who Jesus Christ was and why and how He would, or could, take upon Himself our sins and sorrows. She also grew up believing sin always brought punishment, borne by us alone. She asked God to help her understand divine forgiveness. She prayed to know how Jesus Christ can forgive those who repent, how mercy can satisfy justice.

One day her prayer was answered in an unexpected way. While shopping, she saw a young man desperately running with two bags of food he had just stolen from a grocery store. The store manager chased and caught the young man. In the busy street, the young man and store manager yelled and fought. My friend's heart filled with compassion for the frightened young man. In a way that surprised her, she approached the two quarreling men. She pled, "I will pay for the food. Please let him go. Please let me pay for the food."

Prompted by the Holy Ghost and filled with a love she

As we offer the miracle of

His grace and forgiveness

to each other, the mercy we

receive and the mercy we

offer can help make life's

injustices just.

HE FORGIVES

had never felt before, my friend said, "All I wanted to do was to help and save the young man." This was a transformative spiritual experience for my friend. She said, "In my heart, I began to feel how and why with pure and perfect love Jesus Christ would willingly sacrifice to be my Redeemer. And why I wanted Him to be my Savior."[9]

No wonder we sing:

> *See, the Good Shepherd is seeking,*
> *Seeking the lambs that are lost,*
> *Bringing them in with rejoicing,*
> *Saved at such infinite cost.*[10]

STRENGTH TO FORGIVE THROUGH CHRIST

Our joy becomes full as we understand the Lamb of God is full of grace and forgiveness. As we offer the miracle of His grace and forgiveness to each other, the mercy we receive and the mercy we offer can help make life's injustices just.[11]

Sometimes life tests our trust in Christ's mercy, justice, and judgment and in His liberating invitation to allow His Atonement to heal us as we forgive others and ourselves.

I once met a woman who had applied to work as a journalist, but the official who assigned jobs was deliberately cruel to her. He denied her request and pointedly told her, "With

THE SHEPHERD AND THE LAMB

my signature, I guarantee you will not become a journalist but will dig sewers." One can imagine what she faced as the only woman digging sewers in a gang of men.

Years later, the political situation in her country changed dramatically and this woman became a government official. One day a man came in needing her signature for a job.

She asked, "Do you remember me?" He did not.

She said, "You do not remember me, but I remember you. With your signature, you guaranteed I never became a journalist. With your signature, you sent me to dig sewers, the only woman in a gang of men."

She told me, "I feel I should treat that man better than he treated me—but I do not have that strength." Often the strength to forgive is not within us, but it can be found in the Atonement of Jesus Christ. When trust is betrayed, dreams shattered, hearts broken and broken again; when we want justice and need mercy; when our fists clench and our tears flow; when we need to know what to hold onto and what to let go of, we can trust the Lamb of God. Innocent, without spot and without blemish, the Lamb of God descended below all things. He now pleads with God our Father for us and those around us as we forgive and are forgiven in and through Him.

HE FORGIVES

As the Golden Rule[12] teaches, a sanctifying symmetry in repentance and forgiveness invites us to offer others that which we ourselves need and desire. Sometimes our willingness to forgive someone else enables both them and us to believe we can repent and be forgiven. Sometimes a willingness to repent and an ability to forgive come at different times. The Lamb of God is our Mediator with God; the Lamb of God also brings us to ourselves and each other as we come to Him. Especially when hurt and pain are deep, repairing our relationships and healing our hearts is hard, perhaps impossible on our own. But heaven can give us strength and wisdom beyond our own to know when to hold on and how to let go.

We are less alone when we realize we are not alone. "Bruised for our iniquities," the Lamb of God always understands.[13] "With his stripes we are healed."[14] With our Savior's help, we can surrender our pride, our hurts, our sins to God. However we may feel as we begin, we become more whole as we trust Him to make us and our relationships whole.

The Lamb of God assures, "He who has repented of his sins, the same is forgiven, and I, the Lord, remember them no more." The Lord also tells us how to know we have repented—we have confessed our sins when needed and

A sanctifying symmetry in repentance

and forgiveness invites us to offer others

that which we ourselves need and desire.

Sometimes our willingness to forgive

someone else enables both them and us to

believe we can repent and be forgiven.

HE FORGIVES

forsaken them.[15] Sometimes, when the Lord says He forgives us, we need to believe Him and forgive ourselves. We may for a period remember what happened, but once we have repented, we can let the past fade. Mercifully, we need not repeatedly bring up past mistakes or call them to the attention of others.

The Lord sees and understands perfectly. He forgives whom and when He will. We, being imperfect, are to forgive all.[16] As we come to our Savior, we focus less on ourselves. We judge less and forgive more. He frees us from contention, anger, abuse, abandonment, unfairness, and the physical and mental challenges that come with mortality. Not every earthly relationship we have will be repaired or happy, but a thousand millennial years when Satan is bound[17] will give us needed time and surprising ways to love, understand, and work things out as we prepare for eternity.

BOTH SIDES OF THE VEIL

"Infinite and eternal,"[18] "stronger than the cords of death,"[19] Jesus Christ's Atonement can bring peace to our past and hope to our future.

Change and repentance, healing and reconciliation, can

THE SHEPHERD AND THE LAMB

occur on both sides of the veil. Atonement—at-one-ment—comes as we exercise faith and bring forth "fruit unto repentance."[20] Through the Atonement of Jesus Christ, the living and "the dead who repent will be redeemed, through obedience to the ordinances of the house of God."[21] In the spirit world, even those in sin and transgression have opportunity to repent.[22]

By permission, I share a sacred, unusually spiritually direct experience a friend shared with me about Jesus Christ uniting families by healing intergenerational conflict. When they joined The Church of Jesus Christ of Latter-day Saints, my friend and her husband gratefully learned family relationships need not be "until death do you part." In the house of the Lord, families can be united eternally (sealed).

But my friend did not want to be sealed to her father. "He was not a nice husband to my mother. He was not a nice dad to his children," she said. "My dad will have to wait. I do not have any desire to do his temple work and be sealed with him in eternity."

For a year, she fasted, prayed, and spoke a lot with the Lord about her father. Finally, she was ready. Her father's temple work was completed. Later, she said, "In my sleep my dad appeared to me in a dream, all dressed in white. He had

74

HE FORGIVES

changed. He said, 'Look at me. I am all clean. Thank you for doing the work for me in the temple.'" Her father added, "Get up and go back to the temple; your brother is waiting to be baptized."

My friend says, "My ancestors and those that have passed on are eagerly waiting for their work to be done."

"As for me," she says, "the temple is a place of healing, learning, and acknowledging the Atonement of Jesus Christ."

Peace and healing come as we let go of hurt and trauma through Jesus Christ. This includes as we offer others the opportunity to make sacred temple covenants with the Lord. As we come meekly and lowly to the Lamb of God, He who understands everything can make everything right.

Especially when we forgive and reconcile together, we find strength in the divine reality that He forgives—each of us, and each of us together. We praise the Lord and express deepest gratitude: "Hosanna to God and the Lamb!"[23]

CHAPTER 7

HE DELIVERS AND REDEEMS

In ancient Israel, the scapegoat ceremonially took the sins and faults of the people and carried them out of the camp into the wilderness.[1] This symbolic tradition anticipates how, with patience and love, Jesus Christ can deliver and redeem us from bondage and captivity. This includes from our foibles and faults, arrogance and ignorance, willfulness and pride, sins and mistakes, unintended hurts and spiteful misuse of each other.

DELIVERANCE AND PASSOVER

In the Old Testament, the Lord delivers the children of Israel from four hundred years of bondage. Jewish tradition celebrates this deliverance as Passover. The book of Exodus describes plagues of frogs, lice, flies, the death of cattle, boils, blains, hail and fire, locusts, and thick darkness. The final plague threatened the death of the firstborn in each family except those in the house of Israel *if*—if those households put the blood of an unblemished firstling lamb on their door lintels.[2]

Scripture records that the angel of death passed by the houses marked with the symbolic blood of the lamb.[3] That passing by, or "pass over," represents Jesus Christ's deliverance and redemption, ultimately including from death. Indeed, the atoning blood of the Lamb of God offers to deliver and redeem all on both sides of the veil into the safety of His fold.

How grateful we are for certain assurance that precious family relationships can be perpetuated beyond the grave and families can be united eternally.[4]

Our family felt those assurances and covenant blessings as we retraced the steps and dedicated the graves of Thomas and Mary Franks Cunningham. Available records indicate Thomas Cunningham was born in Ireland, in County Galway. In the mid-nineteenth century, Ireland's potato blight decimated Ireland's staple food. "The Great Hunger" sent millions in search of survival, Thomas Cunningham among them. Thomas moved to Loughborough, England,

HE DELIVERS AND REDEEMS

where he lived near the canal lined with bulrushes. The area is still called the Rushes. In 1851, he and his future wife, Mary Franks, were neighbors, living only minutes apart by walking. In 1853, they were married at St. Mary's Church when the original altar was at the front. Illiterate, they each signed their marriage document with an "X." Their first child, John, died as a toddler and is likely buried in the St. Mary's Church cemetery.

Thomas and Mary Franks Cunningham had a daughter, whom they named Mary Ann. Baptized at age eleven, Mary Ann crossed the plains with the early Church pioneers. She is one of Sister Gong's great-grandmothers. For more than 150 years, the bodies of Thomas and Mary Cunningham lay in unmarked paupers' graves in the Loughborough Cemetery. With the help of FamilySearch missionaries, our family was able, for the first time, to locate Thomas's and Mary's graves and to mark them with a granite headstone. As their graves were dedicated and consecrated, we prayed the Lord to hallow and protect where Thomas and Mary are buried awaiting the Resurrection.

As we stood in a family circle that day in Loughborough, Jesus Christ's overcoming death and His promise of deliverance and redemption were very real for us. In the eyes of the

79

In the eyes of the world, we

may be considered of little

notice or worth. . . . But we are

not unvalued or unknown or

forgotten in the heart of the Lamb

of God. He redeems and delivers

even the least of us.

world, we may be considered of little notice or worth—illiterate, buried in an unmarked pauper's grave after suffering tuberculosis and dying in a workhouse. But we are not unvalued or unknown or forgotten in the heart of the Lamb of God. He redeems and delivers even the least of us.

We can be united by covenant in Jesus Christ and belong together as families eternally.

FOR SUCH A TIME AS THIS

Father Abraham, who established covenant blessings for all the nations of the earth, experienced what it meant to offer his begotten son. "And Isaac spake unto Abraham his father, and said, My father: and he said, Here am I, my son. And he said, Behold the fire and the wood: but where is the lamb . . . ? And Abraham said, My son, God will provide himself a lamb."[5]

In our lives, are there times when we need and find a God-given ram in the thicket?

Jewish tradition honors Esther, who was raised up "for such a time as this."[6] As we recall, Queen Esther found herself in a perilous situation. Her life was at risk if she intervened to save the lives of her people, who otherwise would all be lost. The story begins when King Ahasuerus seeks a queen and chooses Esther, a maid "fair and beautiful," who had "obtained favour in the sight of all them that looked upon her."[7] Esther had been raised by her uncle Mordecai, who had charged her to not disclose she was a Jew.

Haman, advanced by the king to a "seat above all the princes that were with him,"[8] grew full of wrath when Mordecai did not bow when Haman passed or show him reverence. In his anger at Mordecai, Haman plotted to destroy all the Jews. In desperation for himself and their people, Mordecai famously told Esther, "Who knoweth whether thou art come to the kingdom for such a time as this?"[9] In the end, it is Haman who is hanged on the gallows he had had made to hang Mordecai, a gallows fifty cubits high.[10]

Esther was willing to be found in the right place, at the right time, to bless those around her. In His infinite and eternal way, our Savior and Redeemer, the Lamb of God, stands ready to bless us in the myriad circumstances of our life's journey, including for such a time as this.

LIBERATING THE CAPTIVES

Another dimension to Jesus Christ as Deliverer and Redeemer comes from His comforting mission to liberate the captives.[11]

HE DELIVERS AND REDEEMS

I remember the steel doors closing behind me as I entered the state penitentiary to meet the inmates. I was surprised to find the inmates wearing white jumpsuits. I instinctively thought of other groups dressed in white. Indeed, Jesus Christ comes to deliver the penitent from prison. He helps us change our hearts, countenances, character. Dressed in penitent, spiritual-prison white, as it were, we can each come to Jesus Christ ready to dress in temple white, prepared for eternal ordinances.

On another occasion, I visited prison inmates at Christmastime. A skilled pianist, one inmate offered to play Christmas songs. The group asked to sing "Rudolph the Red-Nosed Reindeer," "Frosty the Snowman," "Silent Night," and "O Little Town of Bethlehem." Everyone, it seems, feels nostalgic at Christmas. We spoke of the babe at Bethlehem, the Lamb of God whose way, truth, and life can liberate the captives.

> WITH THE FAITHFUL USE OF OUR AGENCY AND THE ENABLING POWER OF THE ATONEMENT OF THE LAMB OF GOD, WE CAN FIND PEACE, EVEN WITH OUR MOST TROUBLED PASTS, AND HOPE, EVEN IN OUR MOST UNCERTAIN FUTURES.

THE SHEPHERD AND THE LAMB

Though all sin, all can have hope in Jesus Christ.[12] His deliverance and redemption come in time and eternity. Perfectly, He measures and discerns our heart and character.

As in this life, so in the next life. Temple ordinances, including baptism, do not of themselves change us or those in the spirit world. But these divine ordinances enable sanctifying covenants with the Lord. With the faithful use of our agency and the enabling power of the Atonement of the Lamb of God, we can find peace, even with our most troubled pasts, and hope, even in our most uncertain futures.

The Lamb of God delivers and redeems. In all things, He invites and brings us to Him and God, our Eternal Father, through relationships that last in time and eternity—through covenant belonging.

CHAPTER 8
HE COVENANTS

Jesus Christ, the Lamb of God, makes covenant belonging possible. By His nature, God "keepest covenant and showest mercy."[1] His covenants endure "so long as time shall last, or the earth shall stand, or there shall be one man upon the face thereof to be saved."[2] Centered in the Lamb of God, covenant relationships help bring God's children home. *Salvation*, *redemption*, and *happiness* are three of the scriptural names for God's divine plan for us. Salvation, redemption, and enduring celestial happiness are possible because the Lamb of God "wrought out this perfect atonement."[3]

The song of our risen Savior's redeeming love celebrates the harmony of covenants, which connect us to God and to each other, and of the Atonement of Jesus Christ, which helps us put off the natural man and woman and yield to the sanctifying "enticings of the Holy Spirit."[4]

That harmony is expressed in God's loving plan of happiness, in which we learn and grow by daily exercise of individual moral agency. We are not left to journey on our own but are given profound gospel teachings to teach us, commandments to protect us, a covenant path to guide us, and the gift of the Holy Ghost to bless us. With us in the beginning, Jesus Christ promises to be with us to the end, when "God shall wipe away all tears from [our] eyes,"[5] except our tears of joy.

TOGETHER, OUR COVENANTS AND OUR SAVIOR'S ATONEMENT CAN SHAPE WHAT WE DESIRE, PERCEIVE, AND EXPERIENCE IN DAILY MORTALITY AND PREPARE US FOR THE SOCIALITY OF HEAVEN.

The harmony of our covenants and the Atonement of Jesus Christ is heard in the melodies and descants as our Savior's Atonement helps us fulfill our covenants in new and holier ways. Together, our covenants and our Savior's Atonement can shape what we desire, perceive, and experience in daily mortality and prepare us for the sociality of heaven.[6]

HE COVENANTS

COVENANT BELONGING

I call our covenant bonds "covenant belonging." Jesus Christ is our "mediator of the new covenant."[7] He came as "an high priest of good things to come, by a greater and more perfect tabernacle. . . . Neither by the blood of goats and calves, but by his own blood he entered in once into the holy place, having obtained eternal redemption for us."[8] Those who shall come forth in the Resurrection of the just include men and women "made perfect through Jesus the mediator of the new covenant, who wrought out this perfect atonement through the shedding of his own blood."[9]

The Book of Mormon is evidence we can hold in our hand of covenant belonging. The Book of Mormon is the promised instrument for the gathering of God's children, prophesied as a new covenant.[10] As we read the Book of Mormon, by ourselves and with others, silently or aloud, we can ask God "with a sincere heart, with real intent, having faith in Christ," and receive "by the power of the Holy Ghost" a witness from God that the Book of Mormon is true,[11] that Jesus Christ is our Savior, that Joseph Smith is the Prophet of the Restoration, and that the fullness of the gospel of Jesus Christ and His Church have been restored.

The Book of Mormon speaks by ancient and modern

Covenant belonging refines. It comes early and stays late. It is unselfish. It works miracles. It gives voice to His love in time and eternity.

HE COVENANTS

covenant to each of us, including to the children of Lehi, "children of the prophets."[12] Your forefathers received a covenant promise that their descendants would recognize in the Book of Mormon a voice "crying from the dust."[13] The testimony you feel as you read witnesses that you are "children of the covenant."[14] Jesus is your Good Shepherd, the Lamb of God.

Covenant belonging is a miracle. It is not possessive. Like charity, it "suffereth long, and is kind." It "envieth not; . . . vaunteth not itself, is not puffed up."[15] Covenant belonging gives roots and wings. It liberates through commitment. It enlarges through love. It opens every possibility.

Covenant belonging refines. It comes early and stays late. It is unselfish. It works miracles. It gives voice to His love in time and eternity.

COVENANT BLESSINGS

Restored priesthood authority with power to bless all His children is another dimension of covenant belonging. In this dispensation, John the Baptist and the Apostles Peter, James, and John came as glorified messengers from God to restore His priesthood authority.[16] When exercised with gentleness, meekness, and love unfeigned,[17] God's priesthood and His

91

ordinances sweeten relationships on earth and can seal covenant relationships in heaven.[18] Priesthood can bless literally from cradle to grave—from an infant's name and blessing to a grave dedication.

Have you noticed that while baptism and other sacred ordinances are outwardly the same for each of us, they call and personally connect us by our individual name with the sacred name of Jesus Christ? God's ordinances and covenants are universal in their requirement and individual in their opportunity. In God's fairness, all can receive saving ordinances. But agency applies—each individual can choose whether to enter into the covenants the ordinances offer.

SANCTIFIED BY COVENANT

God's ordinances provide guideposts on His path of covenants. When we are "sanctified in Christ . . . in the covenant of the Father,"[19] all things can work together for our good. As we honor our covenants, we may sometimes feel we are in the company of angels. And we will be—those who love and bless us on this and the other side of the veil.

In covenant belonging, we strengthen each other in our Savior's love, thereby coming to love God and each other more. Covenant belonging "seeketh not her own, is not easily provoked, thinketh no evil." Covenant belonging "rejoiceth not in iniquity, but rejoiceth in the truth."[20] Covenant belonging is to come and see face to face, knowing even as we are known.[21] Our covenant faithfulness can become "steadfast and immovable."[22]

Covenant belonging is to hope all things, endure many things, and "hope to be able to endure all things."[23] Covenant belonging is to keep the faith. It is not to give up on ourselves, on each other, nor on God.

Covenant belonging is to delight with those who delight and to rejoice with those who rejoice. It is to bear one another's burdens, to mourn with those who mourn, to comfort those who stand in need of comfort.[24] It is to stand as witnesses of God's tender mercies and daily miracles "at all times and in all things, and in all places."[25]

Meant to be eternal, our covenants include God, our Eternal Father, and His Son, Jesus Christ. Eternal covenants can bring the power of God's love—to give hope and increase love; to lift and transform; to edify and sanctify; to redeem and exalt.

In this way, by covenant and belonging in Him, we can each be strengthened in His love as the sheep of His fold and pasture.

CONCLUSION
HOSANNA AND HALLELUJAH

With hosanna and hallelujah, we celebrate the living Jesus Christ—the Shepherd and the Lamb.

When the deep feelings of our heart and soul well up and cannot be contained, we shed tears of joy or tears of pain.

We spontaneously exclaim in praise and petition in prayer.

When we cannot but praise, we shout, "Hallelujah"—literally, "Praise ye the Lord."[1]

When we cannot but pray, we plead, "Hosanna"—literally, "Save now."[2]

Jesus Christ lives—not only then, but now; not just for some, but for all. He calls, gathers, ministers, and strengthens.

He restores, forgives, delivers and redeems, and covenants. As we come to Jesus Christ, His redeeming promises offer hope, no matter our past, our present, or concerns for our future. He is our hosanna and hallelujah.

HOLY WEEK

Traditionally, we associate *hosanna* and *hallelujah* with Holy Week—the events and promises from Palm Sunday to Easter Sunday. This final week of Jesus Christ's mortal ministry include His Atonement and glorious Resurrection. These sacred events are the story of hosanna and hallelujah.

Palm leaves are a traditional, sacred symbol to express joy in our Lord. At Jesus's triumphal entry into Jerusalem, "much people . . . took branches of palm trees, and went forth to meet him."[3] Hosanna and hallelujah also remind us that each day that passes from His prophesied triumphal entry into Jerusalem[4] brings us a day closer to His promised Second Coming, when we will again shout, "Hosanna!"

Of course, the significance of Palm Sunday goes beyond crowds greeting Jesus with palms. On Palm Sunday, the faithful recognized Jesus entering Jerusalem as fulfillment of prophecy. As Zechariah prophetically foretold, our Lord

As we come to Jesus Christ,

His redeeming promises offer

hope, no matter our past, our

present, or concerns for our

future. He is our hosanna

and hallelujah.

entered the Holy City riding a colt as multitudes knowingly cried "Hosanna in the highest."[5]

In biblical times, the Feast of the Tabernacles featured shouts of "hosanna." Such declarations were also included at the special Feast of the Tabernacles when Solomon's temple was opened. Psalm 118, verses 25–26, is a traditional chiasmatic pattern of prayer and praise: "Save now, I beseech thee, O Lord: O Lord, I beseech thee, send now prosperity." Then as now, we rejoice, "Blessed be he that cometh in the name of the Lord."

In the book of Revelation, those who praise God and the Lamb do so "clothed with white robes, and palms in their hands."[6] The March 27, 1836, Kirtland Temple dedicatory prayer likewise looks forward to the day when we "may ever be with the Lord," with pure garments, "clothed upon with robes of righteousness, with palms in our hands, and crowns of glory upon our heads."[7]

A week following Palm Sunday is Easter Sunday. Easter Sunday marks a pivotal point, central in time and eternity, in God's eternal plan of happiness. Easter marks the triumphal fulfillment of Jesus Christ's life, ministry, and divine mission, culminating in His Atonement and Resurrection and all they imply and encompass.

HOSANNA AND HALLELUJAH

SINGING SONGS OF PRAISE

Many sacred hymns give heartfelt voice to "alleluia" and "hallelujah," two spellings of the same word with the same meaning—"Praise ye the Lord Jehovah."[8]

In the beloved hymn, "All Creatures of Our God and King," we lift up our voice and sing, "Alleluia! Alleluia!"[9]

In the triumphal hymn, "Press Forward, Saints," "with steadfast faith in Christ," we exclaim, "Alleluia! Alleluia! Alleluia!"[10]

With our children, we sing,

> *Sleep, little Jesus. . . .*
> *Heavenly hosts sing, "Alleluia,*
> *Peace to all men, Alleluia!"*[11]

In the Christmas carol, "Silent Night," we remember

> *Heav'nly hosts sing Alleluia!*
> *Christ, the Savior, is born!*[12]

At Easter, "Christ the Lord Is Risen Today" is one of my personal favorites. "Alleluia!" punctuates all twelve lines of this hymn, beginning with

> *Christ the Lord is ris'n today, Alleluia!*
> *Sons of men and angels say, Alleluia!*

THE SHEPHERD AND THE LAMB

Raise your joys and triumphs high, Alleluia!
Sing, ye heav'ns, and earth reply, Alleluia![13]

Of course, the "Hallelujah Chorus" in George Frideric Handel's *Messiah* is beloved as an exuberant Easter and Christmas declaration that He is "King of kings, and Lord of lords."[14] Oxford University's Bodleian Library preserves Handel's original *Messiah* conducting score. Complete with his handwritten notes, this is the score Handel used when he first conducted the *Messiah* in Dublin on April 13, 1742. Fittingly, the proceeds from that first *Messiah* performance were used to pay the debts and to free those held in a debtor's prison.[15] As President Russell M. Nelson succinctly observed, "Jesus Christ came to pay a debt He didn't owe, because we owed a debt we couldn't pay."[16]

In many places, the tradition of the "Hallelujah Chorus" includes the audience spontaneously rising to its feet (as tradition says King George II did at the *Messiah*'s 1743 London premiere) in heartfelt exclamation of "Hallelujah!" As I count them, the "Hallelujah Chorus" declares *hallelujah* in unison, counterpoint, and harmony twenty-three times. Often it feels like even more because we feel heavenly voices join our earthly voices in praising the Lord Jehovah.

HOSANNA AND HALLELUJAH

SHOUTS OF HOSANNA

In addition to Easter and Christmas, there are other special times when we cannot but exclaim, "Save now!" and "Praise the Lord!"

These exclamations are reminiscent of the grand premortal council in heaven, "when the morning stars sang together, and all the sons [and daughters] of God shouted for joy."[17] These declarations may portend, as President Lorenzo Snow taught, the Hosanna Shout that will herald the Second Coming of the Messiah.[18]

In the New World, as the Book of Mormon preciously records, the resurrected Jesus Christ invited the multitude to come put their hands into His side. One by one, they felt and witnessed the prints of the nails in His hands and feet. They knew "of a surety and [bore] record, that it was he, of whom it was written by the prophets, that should come." All cried out with one accord, saying, "Hosanna! Blessed be the name of the Most High God!"[19]

In our latter-day dispensation, Restoration scripture includes joyful instruction to declare truth "with a sound of rejoicing, crying—Hosanna, hosanna, blessed be the name of the Lord God!"[20] Similar instruction appears in Doctrine and Covenants 36:3 ("Declare it with a loud voice, saying:

101

Hosanna, blessed be the name of the most high God") and Doctrine and Covenants 39:19 ("Go forth, crying with a loud voice, saying: The kingdom of heaven is at hand; crying: Hosanna! blessed be the name of the Most High God.")

With hallelujah in our heart, we shout hosanna to God and the Lamb on special, sacred occasions.

The Hosanna Shout was first performed by the Church during the March 27, 1836, dedication of the Kirtland Temple. (It was again performed three days later, on March 30, 1836, during the solemn assembly in the newly dedicated house of the Lord.)[21] The Kirtland Temple dedicatory prayer concludes with the petition that "by the power of thy Spirit" the congregation may mingle its voices with heavenly hosts "with acclamations of praise, singing Hosanna to God and the Lamb!"[22] Instead of palms, participants in the Hosanna Shout waved white handkerchiefs.[23]

Following the Hosanna Shout, the congregation burst forth in the hymn "Hosanna to God and the Lamb," known today as "The Spirit of God." Joyfully echoing the Hosanna Shout, the early Saints chorused,

> *We'll sing and we'll shout with the armies of heaven,*
> *Hosanna, hosanna to God and the Lamb!*[24]

To this day, in joyous heartfelt unison, we conclude temple dedications with the Hosanna Shout and "The Spirit of God." Literally, we sing and we shout. We shout praise to God and the Lamb. We sing,

Let glory to them in the highest be given,
Henceforth and forever, Amen and amen![25]

I love that the joyous "Hosanna! Hosanna! Hosanna!" can praise God and the Lamb with full volume and full reverence at the same time.

Shouts of hosanna were also given on other celebratory occasions in early Church history. For example, Brigham Young and Heber C. Kimball led their camps in loud cheers of hosanna to express joy and gratitude for the safe return of Zion's Camp and the Mormon Battalion. Shouts of hosanna were part of early Church solemn assemblies, the ordination of the Seventy, the departure and arrival of the Twelve on missions in England, the capstone and dedication of the Nauvoo Temple, and so on.

On April 6, 1892, by assignment of the First Presidency, President Lorenzo Snow, then President of the Quorum of the Twelve Apostles, led the tens of thousands of Saints gathered for the capstone ceremony of the Salt Lake Temple in the Hosanna Shout. President Snow explained, "We wish the Saints to feel when they pronounce this shout that it comes from their hearts. Let your hearts be filled with thanksgiving."[26]

Exactly a year later, on April 6, 1893, President Wilford Woodruff dedicated the Salt Lake Temple. The Hosanna Shout and "The Spirit of God" were a sacred concluding part of the dedication of the Salt Lake Temple.[27]

At the April 1930 general conference, President Heber J. Grant led the assembled congregation in the Hosanna Shout to celebrate the one-hundredth anniversary of the organization of the Church.[28]

Marking a new millennium, President Gordon B. Hinckley led the Church in the Hosanna Shout when the Conference Center was dedicated on October 8, 2000.[29]

President Russell M. Nelson led Church members around the world in the Hosanna Shout during the Sunday morning session of general conference on April 5, 2020.[30] That April Sunday was a Palm Sunday.

That 2020 Church general conference also marked the beginning of a bicentennial decade which encompasses a series of two-hundred-year anniversaries. These include the two-hundred-year anniversary of the Prophet Joseph Smith's

In the daily details of small and simple things, we can see great things brought to pass in our lives and in the unfolding blessings of God's children everywhere because of the Shepherd and the Lamb.

THE SHEPHERD AND THE LAMB

First Vision, the coming forth of the Book of Mormon by the gift and power of God, the formal restoration and establishment of The Church of Jesus Christ of Latter-day Saints, and much more.

I testify of God, our Eternal Father, and His Only Begotten Son, Jesus Christ, the Shepherd and the Lamb. Mortal men, once cruelly crucified, will be resurrected in unscarred bodies bearing no marks. But only the living Jesus Christ in His perfect, resurrected, and glorified body still bears the marks of His crucifixion in His hands, feet, and side. These marks testify of Him. They fulfill prophecy. They are part of His perfection. Jesus Christ tenderly testifies, "I have graven thee upon the palms of my hands."[31] He witnesses, "I am he who was lifted up. I am Jesus that was crucified. I am the Son of God."[32]

In the daily details of small and simple things, we can see great things brought to pass in our lives and in the unfolding blessings of God's children everywhere because of the Shepherd and the Lamb.[33] "And it shall come to pass that the righteous shall be gathered out from among all nations, and shall come to Zion, singing with songs of everlasting joy."[34]

At every season of hosanna and hallelujah, we sing, "Hallelujah"—for He shall reign forever and ever!

HOSANNA AND HALLELUJAH

At every season of hosanna and hallelujah, we shout, "Hosanna, to God and the Lamb!"

Hosanna and hallelujah to the Shepherd and the Lamb!

NOTES

PREFACE

1. See Soren Kierkegaard, journals, volume 4, circa 1843.
2. W. B. Yeats, "The Lake Isle of Innisfree," in *Poetry Foundation*.

INTRODUCTION: THE SHEPHERD AND THE LAMB

1. Psalm 23:1–3.
2. John 10:11.
3. See John 10:15, 17–18.
4. See Doctrine and Covenants 110:2–10.
5. Doctrine and Covenants 110:3; emphasis added.
6. Doctrine and Covenants 110:4.
7. 2 Nephi 31:20.
8. See Micah 6:8; Doctrine and Covenants 11:12.
9. See John 21, including verse 15.
10. 1 Nephi 13:40.
11. John 1:29.
12. See 1 Nephi 11:27, 31–32; 13:34, 40.
13. Mosiah 14:6; see also Isaiah 53:6.
14. Alma 7:7.
15. Alma 7:14–15.
16. See Job 38:7.

NOTES

17. Abraham 3:27.
18. Helaman 6:5.
19. See Revelation 21:27.
20. See Doctrine and Covenants 133:56; Revelation 15:3.
21. See Revelation 19:9; Doctrine and Covenants 58:11. Revelation 7:17: "For the Lamb . . . shall feed them, and shall lead them unto living fountains of waters: and God shall wipe away all tears from their eyes"; Revelation 22:1: The "pure river of water of life, clear as crystal, proceeding out of the throne of God and of the Lamb."
22. Helaman 15:13.
23. Revelation 5:12.
24. Doctrine and Covenants 109:79.

PART ONE: THE GOOD SHEPHERD

1. The very name *Cotswolds* evokes "sheep enclosures" (*cots*) amidst gentle hills (*wolds*). Even today the sheep flocks there are reminiscent of the United Kingdom's historical wealth found in wool.
2. See Luke 2:8.

CHAPTER 1: HE CALLS

1. John 10:3–4.
2. Alma 5:38; see also Alma 5:37, 39, 59–60.
3. See Doctrine and Covenants 58:27–28.
4. Moroni 10:32.
5. See John 14:6.
6. Matthew 11:28.
7. Luke 15:20.
8. Helaman 15:13.
9. See Moroni 7:13; Doctrine and Covenants 8:2–3.
10. 3 Nephi 27:8; emphasis added.
11. 3 Nephi 27:7, 9; emphasis added.
12. See John 10:7–9.
13. See Psalm 23:2.
14. 2 Nephi 26:25.
15. See John 10:10; 14:6.
16. Doctrine and Covenants 132:23–24; see also John 14:3; 17:3.
17. Doctrine and Covenants 101:42.

NOTES

CHAPTER 2: HE GATHERS

1. Isaiah 40:11.
2. See John 10:16.
3. 2 Nephi 26:33.
4. Luke 15:4, emphasis added; see also Doctrine and Covenants 18:15.
5. Ezekiel 34:12.
6. 1 Nephi 22:25.
7. See Hebrews 13:20; see also Jeremiah 31:10; Ezekiel 34:6, 11–14. The prophecies and promises of scattering and covenant gathering are a consistent theme in both ancient and Restoration scripture.
8. John 10:14–15.
9. John 10:16; see also 3 Nephi 15:17.
10. 3 Nephi 15:24; see also 3 Nephi 15:17, 21.
11. See 3 Nephi 15:17; 16:1–3; Doctrine and Covenants 10:59–60.
12. John 17:12; the verse continues: "none of them is lost, but the son of perdition; that the scripture might be fulfilled."
13. Doctrine and Covenants 50:41–42, 44.
14. Alma 7:11–13.
15. Doctrine and Covenants 19:16–19; see also Matthew 26:38–39, 42, 44.
16. Romans 8:26.
17. 3 Nephi 17:17.
18. 3 Nephi 17:21–22.
19. See Doctrine and Covenants 101:64–65. We think of the house of the Lord as a garner—a holy place built up with the name of the Lord for the gathering, harvest, and securing of the Saints to possess eternal life.
20. Doctrine and Covenants 110:16.
21. Malachi 4:5.
22. See Stephen D. Ricks, "The Appearance of Elijah and Moses in the Kirtland Temple and the Jewish Passover," *BYU Studies* 23, no. 4 (1986), 483–86, byustudies.byu.edu.
23. Doctrine and Covenants 86:10; see also Acts 3:19–21.
24. Joseph Smith—History 1:39; in recent years, many have interpreted the specific possessive "their" as referring to our own kith and kin, our own extended family generations.
25. Doctrine and Covenants 128:9.
26. See 2 Nephi 2:8.

NOTES

CHAPTER 3: HE MINISTERS

1. See Acts 10:38.
2. Matthew 25:40; see also 25:35–39.
3. See Mark 12:31.
4. John 13:34.
5. Matthew 20:26; see also Luke 22:26–27.
6. Acts 26:16.
7. See Luke 7:11–15.
8. Matthew 9:36.
9. See Mark 6:31–44.
10. See Mark 5:22–43.
11. Mark 5:26.
12. Luke 8:48; see also Mark 5:24–34; Luke 8:43–48; Matthew 9:20–22.
13. See Luke 5:1–11.
14. See John 21:1–11.
15. See Doctrine and Covenants 8:5.
16. Doctrine and Covenants 11:1.
17. Doctrine and Covenants 11:3.
18. Doctrine and Covenants 11:4.
19. Doctrine and Covenants 11:12.
20. Doctrine and Covenants 11:21.
21. Psalm 80:1.
22. See Ezekiel 34:2–6.
23. See Nahum 3:18.
24. See Jeremiah 23:1; 50:6.
25. See Isaiah 56:11; Ezekiel 34:2–6.
26. John 10:13.
27. 3 Nephi 14:15; see also Matthew 7:15; Alma 5:60.
28. See John 10:2–4.
29. See Russell M. Nelson, "Ministering," *Ensign* or *Liahona*, May 2018, 100.
30. See Moroni 7:47.
31. This theme appears throughout Jacob 5, including in verses 17–18, 20, 24, and 75. Verse 28 reminds us, "The Lord of the vineyard and the servant of the Lord of the vineyard did nourish *all* the fruit of the vineyard" (emphasis added).
32. The Lord of the vineyard asks twice, "What could I have done

NOTES

more *for* my vineyard?" (Jacob 5:41, 49; emphasis added) and once, "What could I have done more *in* my vineyard?" (Jacob 5:47; emphasis added).

33. In the spirit of Mosiah 18:8–9 and Matthew 25:40.

34. Jacob 5:74: "And they became like unto one body; and the fruits were equal"; see also, 1 Corinthians 12:12: "For as the body is one, and hath many members, and all the members of that one body, being many, are one body: so also is Christ."

35. Doctrine and Covenants 64:33; see also Alma 37:34.

36. See Mosiah 4:27.

37. 2 Corinthians 9:7.

38. 2 Corinthians 9:10.

39. 2 Corinthians 9:11.

40. 2 Corinthians 9:6.

CHAPTER 4: HE STRENGTHENS

1. See 2 Nephi 31:18; see also Matthew 7:14.

2. Galatians 6:7.

3. See Doctrine and Covenants 137:1–6.

4. Doctrine and Covenants 137:9; see also verses 7–8, 10. Indeed, as verse 7 says, "All who have died without a knowledge of this gospel, who would have received it if they had been permitted to tarry, shall be heirs of the celestial kingdom of God." Further, the Lord continues, "All that shall die henceforth without a knowledge of it, who would have received it with all their hearts, shall be heirs of that kingdom."

5. Mosiah 2:41.

6. Psalm 37:9.

7. Isaiah 40:31.

8. Mosiah 18:10.

9. See 2 Nephi 31:2, 12–13.

10. See Isaac Watts (1674–1748), "My Shepherd Will Supply My Need," American folk hymn, in *Southern Harmony* (1835).

11. See Matthew 10:39.

12. See Doctrine and Covenants 84:20.

13. See *Lectures on Faith* (1985), 69.

NOTES

CHAPTER 5: HE RESTORES

1. Alma 41:2.
2. Alma 40:23.
3. 1 Corinthians 15:22.
4. Alma 41:4.
5. Alma 41:13.
6. The words *restore, restored, restoration,* or other variants appear twenty-two times in Alma 40:22–24 and in Alma 41, emphasizing both physical and spiritual restoration.
7. Alma 41:14–15; emphasis added.
8. See Ecclesiastes 11:1.
9. Alma 42:15.
10. Alma 7:11.
11. See Alma 7:12.
12. Alma 42:15.
13. 2 Nephi 1:15.
14. Romans 12:21.
15. Romans 12:17, 19.
16. Romans 12:15.
17. John 16:33.
18. See Jacob 2:18–19.

CHAPTER 6: HE FORGIVES

1. Romans 8:35, 38–39.
2. Isaiah 59:2.
3. Alma 34:10.
4. The finest robe, ring, shoes, and even the fatted calf, as it were. See Luke 15:22–23.
5. J. Reuben Clark Jr., in Conference Report, Oct. 1953, 84.
6. Russell M. Nelson, "We Can Do Better and Be Better," *Ensign* or *Liahona*, May 2019, 67.
7. 2 Nephi 25:23.
8. Luke 23:34; see also Matthew 6:12—"forgive us our debts, as we forgive our debtors"—which also relates our ability to be forgiven to our willingness to forgive.
9. Conversation with Pornthip "Tippy" Coyle, Feb. 2019, used with permission.

NOTES

10. "Dear to the Heart of the Shepherd," *Hymns,* no. 221. Other hymns that highlight our Shepherd and His sheep include the following:

> "The Lord My Pasture Will Prepare," *Hymns,* no. 109
> *The Lord my pasture will prepare*
> *And feed me with a shepherd's care.*
> *His presence will my wants supply,*
> *And guard me with a watchful eye.*
> *My noonday walks he will attend*
> *And all my silent midnight hours defend.*
>
> "Help Me Teach with Inspiration," *Hymns,* no. 281
> *Help me find thy lambs who wander;*
> *Help me bring them to thy keep.*
> *Teach me, Lord, to be a shepherd;*
> *Father, help me feed thy sheep.*
>
> "Come, All Ye Sons of God," *Hymns,* no. 322
> *The latter-day work has begun:*
> *To gather scattered Israel in*
> *And bring them back to Zion to praise the Lamb.*
> *Come, all ye scattered sheep, and listen to your Shepherd.*

11. See Alma 42:13–15; see also Robert Frost, "A Masque of Mercy," *Complete Poems of Robert Frost,* ed. Edward Connery Lathem (1969), 521, where Frost writes, "Nothing can make injustice just but mercy."

12. See Matthew 7:12.

13. Isaiah 53:5. "He [was] despised and rejected of men; a man of sorrows, and acquainted with grief" (Isaiah 53:3), but also a Man who gathered the little children and wept with a joy that was full (see 3 Nephi 17:20–24).

14. Isaiah 53:5.

15. Doctrine and Covenants 58:42–43.

16. See Doctrine and Covenants 64:10.

17. See Doctrine and Covenants 43:30–31. We are reminded in 1 Nephi 22:26 that Satan's power will be limited in the Millennium "because of the righteousness of [the Lord's] people."

18. Alma 34:10.

19. Doctrine and Covenants 121:44.

20. Alma 34:30.

NOTES

21. Doctrine and Covenants 138:58.
22. See Doctrine and Covenants 138:32.
23. Doctrine and Covenants 109:79.

CHAPTER 7: HE DELIVERS AND REDEEMS

1. See Leviticus 16:21–22.
2. See Exodus 7–12.
3. See Exodus 12:21–23.
4. See "The Family: A Proclamation to the World," ChurchofJesus Christ.org.
5. Genesis 22:7–8; see also Genesis 22:12–13; Jacob 4:5.
6. Esther 4:14.
7. Esther 2:7, 15.
8. Esther 3:1.
9. Esther 4:14.
10. See Esther 7:9–10.
11. See Jacob 2:19.
12. See Doctrine and Covenants 64:7.

CHAPTER 8: HE COVENANTS

1. Doctrine and Covenants 109:1.
2. Moroni 7:36.
3. Doctrine and Covenants 76:69.
4. Mosiah 3:19.
5. Revelation 7:17.
6. See Doctrine and Covenants 130:2.
7. Hebrews 12:24; Doctrine and Covenants 76:69; 107:19; see also Joseph Smith Translation, Galatians 3:20 (in the Bible appendix).
8. Hebrews 9:11–12.
9. Doctrine and Covenants 76:69.
10. See title page of the Book of Mormon; Doctrine and Covenants 84:57.
11. Moroni 10:4.
12. 3 Nephi 20:25.
13. 2 Nephi 33:13; see also 26:16; Isaiah 29:4.
14. 3 Nephi 20:26.

NOTES

15. 1 Corinthians 13:4; see also Moroni 7:45.
16. See Doctrine and Covenants 13; 27:12; see also introduction to the Doctrine and Covenants.
17. See Doctrine and Covenants 121:41.
18. Doctrine and Covenants 128:8; see also Exodus 19:5–6; Doctrine and Covenants 84:40. Those who worthily keep covenants become a precious treasure, a kingdom of priests and priestesses, a holy nation. Covenants sanctify. Those who keep covenants become sanctified to the Lord.
19. Moroni 10:33; see also Doctrine and Covenants 90:24; 98:3.
20. 1 Corinthians 13:5–6.
21. See 1 Corinthians 13:12.
22. Mosiah 5:15; Alma 1:25.
23. Articles of Faith 1:13; see also 1 Corinthians 13:7; Moroni 7:45.
24. See Mosiah 18:8–9.
25. Mosiah 18:9.

CONCLUSION: HOSANNA AND HALLELUJAH

1. Bible Dictionary, "Hallelujah."
2. Bible Dictionary, "Hosanna."
3. John 12:12–13; see also Matthew 21:8–9; Mark 11:8–10.
4. The original of Harry Andersen's well-known painting *Christ's Triumphal Entry into Jerusalem* (ca. 1970) hangs in the office of the President of the Church, behind the desk.
5. Matthew 21:9; see also Zechariah 9:9.
6. Revelation 7:9.
7. Doctrine and Covenants 109:75–76.
8. See Bible Dictionary, "Hallelujah."
9. "All Creatures of Our God and King," *Hymns*, no. 62.
10. "Press Forward, Saints," *Hymns*, no. 81.
11. "Sleep, Little Jesus," *Children's Songbook*, 47.
12. "Silent Night," *Hymns*, no. 204.
13. "Christ the Lord Is Risen Today!" *Hymns*, no. 200.
14. See George Fridrich Handel (1685–1759), "Hallelujah!" *Messiah* (1741); see also Revelation 17:14.
15. See "The Premier Performance of Handel's Messiah Raised 400 Pounds and Freed 142 Men from Debtor's Prison," The Tabernacle

NOTES

Choir Blog, Mar. 24, 2014, https://www.thetabernaclechoir.org/articles/handel-debtor-prison.html.

16. Russell M. Nelson, in "Handel's Messiah: Debtor's Prison," television, directed by Lee Groberg (Provo, UT: BYU Broadcasting, 2014), available at https://www.churchofjesuschrist.org/media/video/2017-04-0001-handels-messiah-debtors-prison?lang=eng.

17. Job 38:7; see also Lael J. Woodbury, "Hosanna Shout," in *Encyclopedia of Mormonism*, ed. Daniel H. Ludlow (New York: Macmillan, 1992).

18. As quoted in Woodbury, "Hosanna Shout."

19. 3 Nephi 11:13–17.

20. Doctrine and Covenants 19:37.

21. See *Saints: The Story of the Church of Jesus Christ in the Latter Days*, vol. 1, *The Standard of Truth, 1815–1846* (2018), 235–39.

22. Doctrine and Covenants 109:79.

23. See "Temple Dedications and Dedicatory Prayers, Church History Topics, ChurchofJesusChrist.org, accessed June 27, 2023, https://www.churchofjesuschrist.org/study/history/topics/temple-dedications-and-dedicatory-prayers?lang=eng.

24. "The Spirit of God," *Hymns*, no. 2.

25. "The Spirit of God," *Hymns*, no. 2.

26. Lorenzo Snow, in *Teachings of Presidents of the Church: Lorenzo Snow* (2012), 137–39.

27. See *Saints: The Story of the Church of Jesus Christ in the Latter Days*, vol. 2, *No Unhallowed Hand, 1846–1893* (2020), 662–65.

28. See Heber J. Grant, in Conference Report, Apr. 1930, 21–22.

29. See Gordon B. Hinckley, "This Great Millennial Year," *Ensign*, Nov. 2000, 69–70.

30. See Russell M. Nelson, "Hosanna Shout," *Ensign* or *Liahona*, May 2020, 92.

31. Isaiah 49:16; 1 Nephi 21:16.

32. Doctrine and Covenants 45:52.

33. See Alma 37:6.

34. Doctrine and Covenants 45:71.

SCRIPTURE GUIDE

Jesus Christ as the Shepherd

Psalm 23:1–6
Isaiah 40:11
Jeremiah 31:10, 12
Ezekiel 34:11–16
Zechariah 13:7
Matthew 9:36
Matthew 25:31–40
Matthew 26:30–31; see also
    Mark 14:26–28
Mark 6:32–34
Mark 14:26–28
JST Luke 3:4–11
Luke 12:22–32
John 10:1–18, 24–30
John 21:15–17
Hebrews 13:20–21
1 Peter 2:24–25
1 Peter 5:2–4
1 Nephi 13:24–29, 32–41
    (These verses identify Jesus
    Christ as both the Shepherd
    and the Lamb.)
1 Nephi 22:25
Alma 5:37–41, 57–60
Helaman 15:12–13
3 Nephi 15:17, 21–24
3 Nephi 16:1–3
3 Nephi 18:31–32
Mormon 5:17
Doctrine and Covenants 6:34

SCRIPTURE GUIDE

Doctrine and Covenants
10:59–60
Doctrine and Covenants 35:27

Doctrine and Covenants
50:41–44
Doctrine and Covenants 112:14

Jesus Christ as the Lamb

Isaiah 53:1–12
John 1:29, 35–37
Acts 8:31–35
1 Peter 1:18–21
Revelation 5:12–13
Revelation 7:9–10, 14, 17
Revelation 12:11
Revelation 14:1, 3
Revelation 15:3
Revelation 17:14
Revelation 19:7, 9
Revelation 21:22–23, 27
Revelation 22:1, 3–5
1 Nephi 10:10
1 Nephi 11:20–23, 26–36
1 Nephi 12:6–11, 18
1 Nephi 13:24–29, 32–41
(These verses identify Jesus
Christ as both the Shepherd
and the Lamb.)
1 Nephi 14:1–2, 14

2 Nephi 31:4–5
Mosiah 14:1–12
Alma 7:11–14
Alma 13:11–12
Alma 34:36
Helaman 6:5
Mormon 9:6
Ether 13:10–12
Doctrine and Covenants 58:11
Doctrine and Covenants 65:3
Doctrine and Covenants 76:20–
21, 39, 85, 119
Doctrine and Covenants 88:106,
115
Doctrine and Covenants 109:79
Doctrine and Covenants 132:19,
23–24
Doctrine and Covenants 133:18,
56
Moses 7:47

The Lord's People as Shepherds

Jeremiah 23:1–4
Jeremiah 50:6–7
Ezekiel 34:2–6

Acts 20:28–32
Mosiah 18:8–10
Mosiah 26:20–24

Scan the QR code for a message from Elder Gong
and the full text of the scriptures listed in this guide.

ACKNOWLEDGMENTS

Much takes place to make a book like this possible. I express warm appreciation to Lisa Roper, Alison Palmer, and others at Deseret Book, and to Natalie Ethington and Janice LeFevre, all of whom were a delight to work with. This meditation is a personal reflection, not an official Church publication.